too deep for words
DEVOTIONS FOR LENT 2014

AUGSBURG FORTRESS
Minneapolis

TOO DEEP FOR WORDS
Devotions for Lent 2014

ISBN 978-1-4514-7810-5

Writers: David L. Miller (March 5–20), Joelle Colville-Hanson (March 21–
April 4), Mary Hinkle Shore (April 5–19)
Editors: Suzanne Burke, Laurie J. Hanson
Cover design: Laurie Ingram
Interior design: Eileen Engebretson

Manufactured in the U.S.A.

14 13   1 2 3 4 5 6 7 8 9 10

Welcome

Over the centuries, Christians have kept Lent by praying more than usual. To assist you in this traditional Lenten practice, *Too Deep for Words* offers an evocative image, a reading from Paul's letter to the Romans, a quotation to ponder, a reflection, and a prayer for each day's use.

Romans is the thread weaving through this small Lenten companion. It is the New Testament letter read most frequently in worship during this liturgical year (year A of the Revised Common Lectionary). Lent provides a focused time to contemplate texts that may not be preached on frequently. The writers bring their unique voices and pastoral wisdom to these texts, and also offer the voices of other witnesses in the quotations they have chosen in the "To ponder" section for each day.

Images provide another way into these texts. When words may be too deep—or not deep enough—to open the scriptures for you, our hope is that the accompanying image will provoke—evoke—something in you. Wonder about these images. What do they say that words cannot?

As you journey through the days of Lent toward the Easter feast, may *Too Deep for Words* be a worthy companion on the way.

—The editors

March 5 / Ash Wednesday

Romans 1:8-12

First, I thank my God through Jesus Christ for all of you, because your faith is proclaimed throughout the world. For God, whom I serve with my spirit by announcing the gospel of his Son, is my witness that without ceasing I remember you always in my prayers, asking that by God's will I may somehow at last succeed in coming to you. For I am longing to see you so that I may share with you some spiritual gift to strengthen you—or rather so that we may be mutually encouraged by each other's faith, both yours and mine.

To ponder

You stir man to take pleasure in praising you, because you have made us for yourself, and our heart is restless until it rests in you. —Augustine, *Confessions*

Home in the heart

I long to be home. Home is the heart who welcomes and holds us all, the embracing heart of God who draws us into a common sharing of faith and life, love and hope. We all long for home. It is for this sharing in a common heart that God fashioned us.

Paul knows the beauty of such shared community in Christ. On his journeys, he has labored with faithful companions and been lifted by the prayers and gifts of others known only in stories heard and letters received. He longs to see them face-to-face, to touch their faces and bask in the fullness of the heart of love into which Christ has joined them. The ache of incompletion burns in his soul and in ours. We are not complete, not whole, until we are joined with one another, one in the heart of Christ.

The blessing Paul wants to share with the Romans, whom he has never met, is this sheer physical presence. The primary spiritual gift we bring to one another is the warmth of Christ's love in our hearts. It lifts us above ourselves into joy and hope, even in troubling circumstances. It tells us we are home.

Prayer

Let me taste the joyous freedom of home in the love of your people. Amen.

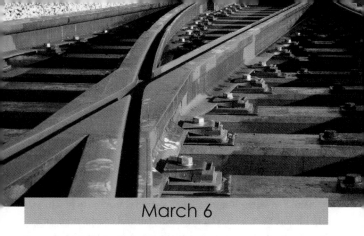

March 6

Romans 2:1, 3-4

Therefore you have no excuse, whoever you are, when you judge others; for in passing judgment on another you condemn yourself, because you, the judge, are doing the very same things. . . . Do you imagine, whoever you are, that when you judge those who do such things and yet do them yourself, you will escape the judgment of God? Or do you despise the riches of his kindness and forbearance and patience? Do you not realize that God's kindness is meant to lead you to repentance?

To ponder

Today, if we have no peace, it is because we have forgotten that we belong to each other—that man, that woman, that child is my brother or my sister. If everyone could see the image of God in his neighbor, do you think we would still need tanks and generals? —Mother Teresa, "Mother Teresa Reflects on Working toward Peace"

Beyond ego

Life is not a competition, although our society's love affair with sports might seem to suggest otherwise. At the heart of much competition is a hunger to feel superior to others. We keep score, counting points or money or accomplishments to prove it, at least to ourselves. Often this masks a hidden self that feels small and weak. The threatened ego rips on others, as if that will lift one above them. There is no peace in this way of living. Every person and situation requires us to prove ourselves again, lest our image slips.

God's kindness invites us to another way, to enter the immensity of divine mercy that embraces all that we are, have been, and ever will be. Our craving to compare and judge evaporates in the warmth of this awareness. Bathed in God's kindness, we can allow others to be as imperfect and needy as we know we are. Our greatest need is to relax and let ourselves be loved by the one who does not condemn us for being human, weak, or sinful. We condemn ourselves when we judge others, for in doing so we are pushing away the Love who leaves no one out in the cold.

Prayer

Water my soul with your immense mercy, that my heart may grow large, with room for all. Amen.

March 7

Romans 7:7-8

What then should we say? That the law is sin? By no means! Yet, if it had not been for the law, I would not have known sin. I would not have known what it is to covet if the law had not said, "You shall not covet." But sin, seizing an opportunity in the commandment, produced in me all kinds of covetousness. Apart from the law sin lies dead.

To ponder

It is God's will that we have most confidence in his delight and love, . . . for just as by God's courtesy he forgets our sin from the time that we repent, just so does he wish us to forget our sins and all our depression and all our doubtful fears. —Julian of Norwich, *Showings*

Hear the voice

A restless anxiety burns in our hearts. We fear we will never taste fulfillment. We crave the sweet inebriation of joy filling our frame and spilling out of us. So we grab at one thing and then another, thinking it is what we need to be whole. Every closed door to our desires is an affront. Deprived of our wants, the first reaction of the fearful, sin-sick heart is to beat down the locked door and grasp what is forbidden, convinced that to be happy and well it must have what is denied.

This dynamic is well known to the mother of any two-year-old, but it doesn't stop there. We are prisoners of this fundamental anxiety, never satisfied, ever grasping at that which imagine will bring fulfillment. This futile game ends only when the voice of total love cuts through our anxiety and says: "Stop it; just stop it. The door to your joy is not locked or bolted. You need not knock it down. Just trust and pull open the door of the future. The one who loves you more than you can comprehend stands on the other side."

Prayer

Lord, let me breathe the air of your love, that with confident hope I may step expectantly into each new day. Amen.

March 8

Romans 7:15-17

I do not understand my own actions. For I do not do what I want, but I do the very thing I hate. Now if I do what I do not want, I agree that the law is good. But in fact it is no longer I that do it, but sin that dwells within me.

To ponder

The mystic path is a journey of personal transformation, and while the goal of the journey is to become our true selves, we can only do this by letting go of who we are not. . . . The mystic does not deny the darkness, in ourselves or in the world, but affirms a light that lies beyond it. And we have faith that the light will prevail because the light is our true identity. Our task is to remember that. —Marianne Williamson, *Everyday Grace*

Who I am

My insides are often a tangled mess. I feel the love of Christ until it flows from my lips in seamless blessing to those who enter my door. Moments later I make snarky comments about someone who frustrates me. In the morning I am strong with hope; by noon every glass my despondent soul sees is at least half empty. So who am I, this strong, grace-filled soul—or the negative heart of petty snark?

And it's not just me. As a nation, we claim to be a people of peace and justice. Then we look the other way as our drones kill innocent children in south Asia. We claim to be caring, while whining about welfare and spending billions we don't have on weapons we will never use. So who are we, one or the other? We are both. And that's good news, hope for our tangled hearts.

The living Spirit of God is at work amid our fears and apathy, selfishness and sin, stirring this confliction of soul, showing us who we are—people being filled with the love of Christ, who is remaking us into the grace he is.

Prayer

Free me from the tangled confusion of my heart that I may live your love. Amen.

Romans 3:19-22a

Now we know that whatever the law says, it speaks to those who are under the law, so that every mouth may be silenced, and the whole world may be held accountable to God. For "no human being will be justified in his sight" by deeds prescribed by the law, for through the law comes the knowledge of sin. But now, apart from law, the righteousness of God has been disclosed, and is attested by the law and the prophets, the righteousness of God through faith in Jesus Christ for all who believe.

To ponder

He is to us everything that is good and comforting and for our help. He is our clothing for he is that love that wraps and enfolds us, embraces us and guides us, surrounds us for his love, which is so tender that he may never desert us. . . . [H]e made everything which is made for love. —Julian of Norwich, *Showings*

The righteousness of God

The sharp tension dividing many North American Christians today involves the character of God. Is God a righteous judge moved by a passion for purity? Or is God an unimaginable love who is filling all creation with the substance of the divine heart? Does God stand far off, looking down on our struggling little lives? Or is God closer than my own breath, seeking to free me from the illusion that I must (or can!) purify my life and make it acceptable to God?

All creation was made by love and in love and for love: I should say Love, the love who is God. God is ever righteous and faithful to the purpose revealed in Christ. In him, created matter and divine Spirit are one harmonious whole. Again and again, the Spirit pours the love of Christ into our leaky hearts, freeing us from prisons of guilt, failure, and unworthiness—and the illusion that God is not for us. God's righteousness does not condemn or confine us but tears open the gates of our prisons that we might live. God is for us—much more than we are for ourselves.

Prayer

Blessed are you, O Lord, and blessed is your holy name, for you love all creation and hate nothing you have made. Amen.

March 10

Romans 3:22b-25, 28

For there is no distinction, since all have sinned and fall short of the glory of God; they are now justified by his grace as a gift, through the redemption that is in Christ Jesus, whom God put forward as a sacrifice of atonement by his blood, effective through faith. . . . For we hold that a person is justified by faith apart from works prescribed by the law.

To ponder

Faith . . . is the experience of God's loving presence, which trusts in God because it is certain it can depend on God. —Grace Adolphsen Brame, *Faith, the Yes of the Heart*

A new day

A fresh breeze floats across the parking lot and fills my senses. Yesterday flies away as I draw in the first breath of spring. Lightness of being fills me, gentle as the morning. My God, how I need this release from the dead weight of winter. And in a moment, with no fanfare, it simply appears, present in the weightless air of early morning, telling me a new day, a new time has dawned. The burden of yesterday is gone. I am free to walk peacefully into this day, filled with the hope that my heart will touch or be found by the Love who made me.

But I'm wrong, again. I do not have to wait to be found. I do not have to search to touch the one who loves me. God has already reached out to me, speaking a language my soul understands.

God has unhooked my soul from the chains of yesterday, freeing me through a love that "ones" us so that all that God is is mine, a loving gift revealed in Christ, that I might live in gentle hope and walk in peace. Even the breeze sings God's name.

Prayer

Set my heart free, Holy One. Whisper your grace in a million ways that my clogged ears might hear and rejoice. Amen.

March 11

Romans 4:13

For the promise that he would inherit the world did not come to Abraham or to his descendants through the law but through the righteousness of faith.

To ponder

My Lord God, I have no idea where I am going. I do not see the road ahead of me. I cannot know for certain where it will end. Nor do I really know myself. . . . I hope that I will never do anything apart from [my] desire [to please you]. And I know that if I do this you will lead me by the right road though I may know nothing about it. —Thomas Merton, *Thoughts in Solitude*

The right road

What did Abraham follow? Did he hear a voice and obey? Was it more like a deep intuition telling him his future was in a distant land unknown to him? Or were things so bad at home that he had to leave and find his own place in the world?

We look askance at people who say they hear voices. Yet how many times have we heard, "I just had a feeling I should do this"? The Spirit finds ways to speak to us, or perhaps I should say *in* us.

However the Spirit spoke to Abraham, he followed the voice on an unlikely journey to a place he'd never seen, trusting God's promise that blessing would come if he'd only follow. I doubt he saw many cairns, trail markers, as he trudged along looking for his new home, but his life is a cairn for us, showing us the right way, the way of faith. He did not know what each day would bring or where he was going. He simply put one foot ahead of the other, trusting that God was guiding him and would fulfill the promise, even on days it didn't seem likely.

Prayer

Grant us the hope that trusts you even when we are lost and alone and don't know where we are going. Amen.

March 12

Romans 4:20-24a

No distrust made [Abraham] waver concerning the promise of God, but he grew strong in his faith as he gave glory to God, being fully convinced that God was able to do what he had promised. Therefore his faith "was reckoned to him as righteousness." Now the words, "it was reckoned to him," were written not for his sake alone, but for ours also.

To ponder

I noted that Abraham himself had been sent into the wilderness, told to leave his father's house also, that this was the narrative of all generations, and that it is only by the grace of God that we are made instruments of his providence and participants in a fatherhood that is always his. —Marilynne Robinson, *Gilead*

Abraham's children

Faces run through my mind sometimes, faces from past and present. Some linger a few moments before another replaces them. Others appear and quickly pass, but they all touch and bless me. These are the faces of my brothers and sisters, fathers and mothers in faith, souls who advised and guided me, who loved and love me still. They are my partners whose presence reminds me that I am not alone. They feel the love I feel and know the one I know.

Somewhere, somehow they tasted the goodness of the heart who calls us from nothingness, breathes life into our flesh, and sends us on the adventure of living. They have tasted and know the goodness of the Lord, and knowing, they, like me, began to trust the one who promises to walk with us every step of our journey, the one who waits with blessing at every destination at which we arrive.

Centuries separate us from Abraham, but we are all his children. Our situation is the same. We go our way trusting the great heart who launched us on life's journey, joined with others who help us keep the faith when we waver.

Prayer

Walk with me this day, Holy One, and send me souls to remind me that I am not alone. Amen.

March 13

Romans 8:1-2

There is therefore now no condemnation for those who are in Christ Jesus. For the law of the Spirit of life in Christ Jesus has set you free from the law of sin and of death.

To ponder

The priest was still on his way, and finally I was bound to voice my deep regret that such delay threatened to deprive my comrade of the final consolations of Our Church. He did not seem to hear me. But a few moments later he put his hand over mine, and his eyes entreated me to draw closer to him. He then uttered these words almost in my ear.... [H]is voice, though halting, was strangely distinct. "Does it matter? Grace is everywhere...." —George Bernanos, *The Diary of a Country Priest*

In the land of Christ

I know in an instant when I leave the sphere of Christ and enter the land of sin and death. My soul grows sad, heavy, and burdened. The land of Christ is freedom and joy, color and light, jubilation and hope. The land of sin and death and that of Christ are not places, unless you think of them as places in the heart. They are modes of awareness and being, and we vacillate between them.

One moment our hearts sag beneath our fears and failures, dashed hopes, sins, and sorrows. Then blessing comes in a ray of sunlight or words of grace and affection, and our souls awaken to the reality that we live in the land of resurrection. Christ lives and speaks in all that is life and all that gives life to our souls, lifting us above all that condemns. There is no condemnation. Say it again; there is no condemnation, no condemnation, no condemnation—none, nothing. It is gone. And when life is hard, when your limits fall fast on your heart, when you grow weary, say it again: There is no condemnation for me. I live in the land of Christ. Christ's grace and life are everywhere.

Prayer

Lift my heart into the land of your resurrection, that I may breathe and live with joy. Amen.

March 14

Romans 8:5-6

For those who live according to the flesh set their minds on the things of the flesh, but those who live according to the Spirit set their minds on the things of the Spirit. To set the mind on the flesh is death, but to set the mind on the Spirit is life and peace.

To ponder

Christian life, living in Christ by the Spirit, is a life in loving communion with God, others, and every living creature. . . . Human persons are created for loving communion with the Father, through Christ, in the Holy Spirit. God is Love, the life that is pouring itself forth. God's very being is the gift of Love, given and giving as gift. —Michael Downey, *Altogether Gift: A Trinitarian Spirituality*

Currents of the Spirit

Where is your Spirit, Holy One, that I may cast my soul into its currents and be lifted into life, knowing the sweet kiss of joy filling me once more? Where shall I go to taste and see your goodness, my soul soaring, carried off by your love?

I retreat to this quiet basement space knowing that your Spirit has found me here in days of struggle and unhappiness, uncertainty and pain. You salve my soul amid the quiet, but you always lead me out into the warmth of this earth to seek the touch of human flesh that connects my heart with the heart of love whom you are.

Is your Spirit within us? Yes, I am sure. I have known its filling and will again. But this divine wind blows also in the space between our hearts, in the emptiness separating one human hand from another. You are this unceasing flow of self-giving love that dances through all life, seeking us in our lonely waywardness. You draw us together to share who and what we are, transforming our flesh into a holy sacrament. When you pull us into your eternal currents, drawing us into each other's arms, we become the image of your heart.

Prayer

Seek and find my heart today, that I may flow in the current of your compassion. Amen.

March 15

Romans 8:9-11

But you are not in the flesh; you are in the Spirit, since the Spirit of God dwells in you. Anyone who does not have the Spirit of Christ does not belong to him. But if Christ is in you, though the body is dead because of sin, the Spirit is life because of righteousness. If the Spirit of him who raised Jesus from the dead dwells in you, he who raised Christ from the dead will give life to your mortal bodies also through his Spirit that dwells in you.

To ponder

This conflict is experienced in every Christian existence as a conflict between a life ensouled by God's Spirit of life and a life which [is] faint-hearted and apathetic. . . . Paul calls the first life "spirit," the second "flesh." . . . Life "in the Spirit" . . . is true life, which is completely and wholly living, life in the divine power of life. —Jürgen Moltmann, *The Source of Life*

Raising the dead

I tried to raise the dead yesterday. I need to do so again today, starting with myself. The Spirit of life and that of death contend daily for our souls, and the listlessness I feel tells me that today's struggle may be more acute. I forget who I am, thinking I am the weariness, the ache, the sadness or discouragement that settles in when my efforts produce little success. But I am wrong, and so was the troubled soul with whom I talked yesterday in my office. He spoke as if he is his failure to find work, as if his losses, wounds, and disappointments define him.

We are not our weakest moments. The Spirit of life dwells in us. We are bearers of Christ crucified and risen. The power of resurrection inhabits our being. This is who you are. For heaven's sake, don't forget it. No, for the sake of your joy and for the sake of every soul you meet today, don't forget it. You are so much more than you think you are. The one who is life lives in you. This is your identity every day and your hope for every tomorrow.

Prayer

Remind me who I am when I forget the power and beauty that dwell in me. Amen.

March 16 / Lent 2

Romans 8:14-15a

For all who are led by the Spirit of God are children of God. For you did not receive a spirit of slavery to fall back into fear, but you have received a spirit of adoption.

To ponder

Any true experience of the Holy gives one the experience of being secretly chosen, invited, and loved. . . . The mystics of all religions talk of being seduced and ravished and of deep inner acceptance, total forgiveness, mutual nakedness, immense and endless gratitude, endless yearning, and always a desire and possibility of more. This is religion at its best and highest and truest. The mystics know themselves to be completely safe and completely accepted at ever deeper levels of trust, exposure, and embrace. . . . This is so different from fear of hell or punishment which characterize so much common religion. —Richard Rohr, *Richard's Daily Meditations*

The smile of knowing

A knowing smile lights the face of the soul sitting across from me, and I know what—make that who—she knows. Her face is rapt in serene happiness and security. Every doubt and fear has been banished by the certitude of the Love who fills her. She knows oneness with God. The Spirit of the Living One fills her spirit as she abides in the divine heart. "It's like an ocean," she says. "I am part of it. It is in me and all around me. Everything is." She feels no separation between her and this infinite expanse of liquid love.

Her words echo the awareness of contemplatives and mystics of every age who experienced the Spirit of adoption, the wonder of being taken in, held and filled by the wonder of the God and Father of our Lord Jesus. All fear disappears, for perfect love drives out all fear. It evaporates the illusion that we are separate and far from God. Without a word, it gives total assurance that we have been taken in, that we belong and always will. This is always true, of course. But there are moments when you just know.

Prayer

Fill my heart with the joy and peace of knowing you, knowing that you want me for this time and forever. Amen.

March 17

Romans 8:15b-17

When we cry, "Abba! Father!" it is that very Spirit bearing witness with our spirit that we are children of God, and if children, then heirs, heirs of God and joint heirs with Christ—if, in fact, we suffer with him so that we may also be glorified with him.

To ponder

My belief is that when you're telling the truth, you're close to God. If you say to God, "I am exhausted and depressed beyond words, and I don't like You at all right now, and I recoil from most people who believe in You," that might be the most honest thing you've ever said. . . . So prayer is our sometimes real selves trying to communicate with the Real, with Truth, with the

Light. It is . . . hoping to be found by a light and warmth . . . instead of darkness and cold. —Anne Lamott, *Help, Thanks, Wow: The Three Essential Prayers*

Windows of grace

It's not articulate or profound, but sometimes, like last Sunday, I look up and say, "Help." Walking from the car to the church door, I didn't want to enter. I felt cold and empty. I would have gladly driven off by myself to drink coffee and avoid all human contact except for the barista. But the fact that I am the pastor—and that it was Sunday—meant something more was expected of me.

An atheist might think my cry-to-the-sky superstitious and childish. And it is childish, I suppose, but it was also the most honest prayer I could offer. And it was exactly what God wanted of me, honesty about the weakness and vulnerability that made running away look attractive. Not only do I think God liked my prayer, I think my one-word cry was not even my prayer. It was God's prayer, God's Spirit speaking in me, drawing me near, inviting me to be as needy as I felt.

Go ahead, the Spirit says. Name it all, and let it all go. I am your Abba, the Loving Spirit who cries out in you, turning your every struggle into a window of opportunity for grace to flow into all your empty places.

Prayer

May every moment of this day be a window for grace to flow into my soul. Amen.

March 18

Romans 8:22-23

We know that the whole creation has been groaning in labor pains until now; and not only the creation, but we ourselves, who have the first fruits of the Spirit, groan inwardly while we wait for adoption, the redemption of our bodies.

To ponder

What with the dazzle of the sky and sun, . . . the soft southern air, and the crowds . . . watching the performance with a delight matched only by . . . the delight of the performing whales, it was as if the whole creation—men and women and beasts and sun and water and earth and sky and, for all I know God himself—was caught up in one great, jubilant dance of unimaginable beauty. And then . . . my eyes were filled with tears . . . because we were given a glimpse of the way life was created to be and is not. —Frederick Buechner, *The Longing for Home*

Aching for eternity

It is not ugliness that makes our souls most ache. It is having known beauty. Nor is it sin and brokenness, hatred or death that hurts the worst. It is having been filled by love and life—and then feeling separated from the source of your joy.

Moments of divine fulfillment come: love floods the heart, and inexhaustible life overflows our being. We taste eternity. But such moments pass, leaving us wanting more of what we have tasted, longing for love, yearning for a world not yet fully born. We sample a sumptuous feast but are denied the main course. This is the ache at the heart of all creation, an ache for the fulfillment of our destiny. We and all things are created in Christ to incarnate—to materialize—Christ's loving and creative spirit.

Just so, we ache and will ache until the Spirit fills every corner of our being, until it saturates every dusty and cast-off corner of creation, until all that is shines with the beauty of the face of Christ. Until the love of Christ fills all things, the Spirit within us will groan, but every pain will bless us, revealing the beauty we are privileged to bear.

Prayer

Move me to lean into the pain of creation. Make my life an instrument of your healing. Amen.

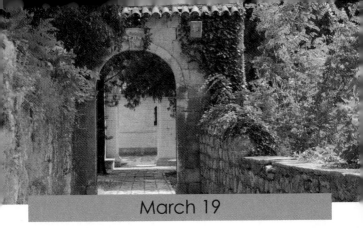

March 19

Romans 8:24-25

For in hope we were saved. Now hope that is seen is not hope. For who hopes for what is seen? But if we hope for what we do not see, we wait for it with patience.

To ponder

Generations have trod, have trod, have trod;
    And all is seared with trade; bleared, smeared with toil;
    And wears man's smudge and shares man's smell. . . .
And for all this, nature is never spent;
    There lives the dearest freshness deep down things;
And though the last lights off the black West went
    Oh, morning, at the brown brink eastward, springs—

Because the Holy Ghost over the bent
   World broods with warm breast and with ah! bright wings.
—Gerard Manley Hopkins, "God's Grandeur"

Waiting for the roses

Early spring: Walking past the rosebushes on the west side of the house, I see buds of red, yellow, and white among the leaves. Finding them, I will them to open, but they pay me no heed. I must wait and hope, even as my heart urges them to break free and sing their colors. Like them, I am moved by a mysterious internal energy to grow and bring beauty from this hidden cavern within me, an unapproachable darkness I don't begin to understand. But I know it is there, and when I stand at its door, waiting in hope, sooner or later beauty and grace appear in my mind and words. I seem to be as possessed of Spirit as are my roses—and as the whole world seems to be, so I hope.

Lord knows, it's not a perfect world. Roses die. None of us have everything we think we need to be happy. And some days I am as much thorn as rose. Still, I walk with hope, knowing the roses will bloom by the side of the house—and in me and the rest of the world too, because that's the way God's Spirit is.

Prayer

Let hope fill my heart and open my eyes to your saving presence. Amen.

March 20

Romans 8:26-27

Likewise the Spirit helps us in our weakness; for we do not know how to pray as we ought, but that very Spirit intercedes with sighs too deep for words. And God, who searches the heart, knows what is the mind of the Spirit, because the Spirit intercedes for the saints according to the will of God.

To ponder

[Thomas] Merton provides us with a unique expression of this concept, in saying: ". . . The best way to pray is: stop! Let prayer pray within you, whether you know it or not. This means a deep awareness of our true inner identity . . . [that] by grace we are Christ. Our relationship with God is that of Christ to the Father in the Spirit." —Thelma Hall, *Too Deep for Words*

Too deep for words

Sometimes I stand in the light on Sunday morning. On spring days, the sun explodes through narrow, angular windows above the front sanctuary wall. I slide up or down the presider's bench so the light envelops me, warming me through even as it blinds me to everything but itself. I look right into it, my heart reaching out to the source of the life-giving rays. Something deep within hungers to bask and live in this circle of light. I don't create or summon this desire. It comes of its own accord.

The Divine Spirit within my mortal flesh moves me beyond myself into wordless prayer, into holiest communion with the Spirit of Light who is infinitely beyond me. Words are unnecessary in such moments. They get in the way of the absolute love that passes back and forth between the divine heart and my own. There is nothing to do or say. The only posture that honors the moment is to savor this union of hearts, this intimation of eternity, and to know: All that is and all that I am rests in the hands of the Loving Mystery revealed in this moment.

Prayer

Fill me with your Spirit and lift me into the joy of wordless communion with you, who are my life, my hope, my all. Amen.

March 21

Romans 8:28
We know that all things work together for good for those who love God, who are called according to his purpose.

To ponder
All shall be well, and all shall be well, and all manner of thing shall be well. —Julian of Norwich, *Revelations of Divine Love*

How do we know?

We know that all things work together for good for those who love God. Do we really know that? Too often I feel like I do not know any such thing. As I face the usual stresses of my own life, never mind the burdens I take on for my children and my congregation, and of course the sadness and tragedies of every night's newscast, I wonder—will all be well?

But then the Holy Spirit stills my deafening scattered thoughts and centers my heart in God, and I realize that of course I know that all things work together for good. I know this but I forget it. I know this but I choose the idolatry of my own worry. And this is why I love the disciplines of Lent that draw me back to the one who has called me according to his purpose. And I know in my quieted heart that all indeed will be well.

Prayer

Dear God, there are times when worries swirl around me, and I need you to remind me of what I know—that in every instance you are there, lovingly and steadfastly bringing all things under your power. Thank you for bringing me back to the hope and knowledge that you are working through all things for good. Amen.

March 22

Romans 8:31-34a

What then are we to say about these things? If God is for us, who is against us? He who did not withhold his own Son, but gave him up for all of us, will he not with him also give us everything else? Who will bring any charge against God's elect? It is God who justifies. Who is to condemn?

To ponder

So when the devil throws your sins in your face and declares that you deserve death and hell, tell him this: "I admit that I deserve death and hell, what of it? For I know One who suffered and made satisfaction on my behalf. His name is Jesus Christ, Son of God, and where He is there I shall be also!" —Martin Luther, *Letters of Spiritual Counsel*

Not wonderful

Who is to condemn me? Actually, I am the one who is most likely to condemn myself. Every day I take inventory, and I always come up short. I don't work as hard as I should. My house isn't as clean as it should be. I don't eat what I should eat. I can't seem to convince as many people to come to church as I would like. I know I'm not as kind and sympathetic as this or that person. I don't pray as much as I should. I'm not as strong, virtuous, or amazing as I wish I were and I think I should be.

Martin Luther said these thoughts come from the devil. They certainly don't come from God. It's not that they aren't true; I have many shortcomings. I am not wonderful. What of it? Christ became human and lived and died and rose again on this earth—for me. Christ didn't come to save wonderful people. He came to bring love, life, and peace to people who are not wonderful. Like you and me.

Prayer

Dear God, I'm not wonderful. And yet you love me anyway. Send your Spirit to make me secure in that knowledge, so that I might turn my thoughts away from self-condemnation and toward loving others who also feel less than wonderful. Amen.

March 23 / Lent 3

Romans 8:35, 38-39

Who will separate us from the love of Christ? Will hardship, or distress, or persecution, or famine, or nakedness, or peril, or sword? . . . For I am convinced that neither death, nor life, nor angels, nor rulers, nor things present, nor things to come, nor powers, nor height, nor depth, nor anything else in all creation, will be able to separate us from the love of God in Christ Jesus our Lord.

To ponder

God is in the slums, in the cardboard boxes where the poor play house. God is in the silence of a mother who has infected her child with a virus that will end both their lives. God is in

40

the cries heard under the rubble of war. God is in the debris of wasted opportunity and lives, and God is with us if we are with them. —Bono, at 2006 National Prayer Breakfast

Fully present

I don't know why our first response to suffering is to ask where God is. Suffering is not a sign of God's absence. This is what the message of the cross is all about. God is with us in the darkest, ugliest, and most painful parts of our lives. God is in the darkest, ugliest, and most painful areas of this world. If we feel God's absence, perhaps it is because we are trying too hard to avoid those dark places.

Where is God in my suffering? God is in the love and kindnesses being shown to me by others, maybe even those I least expect. Where is God in the suffering of others? God is in the compassion and generosity shown by others who respond in love. God is even in my own efforts to reach out to those around me who need love.

Prayer

Dear God, I feel overwhelmed at times by my own difficulties and the suffering I see around me. I need your Holy Spirit to ground me in the conviction that nothing can separate me from you, and when I enter into the pain of others, I experience your presence even more surely. Amen.

March 24

Romans 9:14-16

What then are we to say? Is there injustice on God's part? By no means! For he says to Moses,

"I will have mercy on whom I have mercy,
and I will have compassion on whom I have compassion."

So it depends not on human will or exertion, but on God who shows mercy.

To ponder

Deserves it! I daresay he does. Many that live deserve death. And some that die deserve life. Can you give it to them? Then do not be too eager to deal out death in judgment. For even the very wise cannot see all ends. —J. R. R. Tolkien, *The Fellowship of the Ring*

42

Not fair

Sometimes I think God isn't fair. But the truth is that I'm not fair. I seek mercy for myself, justice for others. I think I deserve the good that comes my way, but I don't deserve the difficulties, even when they are the consequences of my own actions. I'm quick to observe when someone else seems to "get away with it" but conveniently forget how many times I have escaped the consequences of my bad choices.

God is better than fair. God is compassionate and merciful. God is compassionate and merciful to everyone, not just me. But more importantly, *even* me!

Prayer

Dear God, when I get too concerned with the mercy you show others, turn my heart back to the mercy you have shown me. Help me to repent of my jealousy and give only praise and thanks to you for your love and compassion. Amen.

March 25

Romans 9:20-21

But who indeed are you, a human being, to argue with God? Will what is molded say to the one who molds it, "Why have you made me like this?" Has the potter no right over the clay, to make out of the same lump one object for special use and another for ordinary use?

To ponder

It is not you that shapes God, it is God that shapes you. If you are the work of God, await the hand of the artist who does all things in due season. —Irenaeus, *Against Heresies*

Model clay

These words remind me that patience with myself is ultimately patience with God. When I am angry that I am not the person I think God wants me to be, it is because I have forgotten who the potter is, who is shaping me. God is not sitting back waiting for me to get my act together to be the person I should be. God is gently leading and guiding and shaping me through my life's experiences. My task is to trust the hand of the artist. I'm always disappointed when I trust my own ability to become the disciple God is calling me to be.

Grace is to be found when I stop arguing with God about the way I am made. The more I trust the Artist, the more I become the work of God that I am meant to be.

Prayer

Dear God, you are the potter, I am the clay. Grant me grace and patience to appreciate your handiwork in me, to love the person you are shaping me into. Amen.

Romans 10:8-9

But what does it say?
> "The word is near you,
> on your lips and in your heart"

(that is, the word of faith that we proclaim); because if you confess with your lips that Jesus is Lord and believe in your heart that God raised him from the dead, you will be saved.

To ponder

A good head and a good heart are always a formidable combination. —Nelson Mandela, *Long Walk to Freedom*

Lips and heart

It's not enough to just believe something "in your heart." That alone is not faith. When you really believe and trust something, you confess it. You say it out loud, regardless of the consequences. When you really believe that God is stronger than death, stronger than hate, stronger than evil, and you say it out loud—damn the consequences—then evil, hate, and death have no power over you. That is the power of resurrection. That is salvation.

Salvation doesn't just mean you get to go to heaven because you believe in something that happened a few thousand years ago. Salvation is freedom from the fear and despair that keep us from taking on evil things in this world. That is how confessing with your lips and believing in your heart that God raised Jesus from the dead saves us.

Prayer

Dear God, push my faith from my heart to my lips, so I shout your salvation to the world. Amen.

March 27

Romans 10:12-13

For there is no distinction between Jew and Greek; the same Lord is Lord of all and is generous to all who call on him. For, "Everyone who calls on the name of the Lord shall be saved."

To ponder

While I know myself as a creation of God, I am also obligated to realize and remember that everyone else and everything else are also God's creation. —Maya Angelou, *Wouldn't Take Nothing for My Journey Now*

We're all in

I think the root of all sin is our desire to distinguish ourselves from others. We like to draw lines that keep us in and others out. I think the appeal of "reality television" has to do with watching others behaving badly and taking pride that we are "not as bad as those people." I don't know why it isn't enough that God loves me.

There is some mean part of me that wants God to love me and not you. I don't know why that is, but it is as true of me as it is of anyone else.

There is no distinction. We are equal in our capacity for un-kindness. And yet we are equally loved and forgiven by God and equally called by that love to break down those false distinctions.

Prayer

Dear God, you love equally me and those I may look down on. Wash away the lines I draw, and sweep us all together in your one embrace. Amen.

March 28

Romans 10:14-15a

But how are they to call on one in whom they have not believed?
And how are they to believe in one of whom they have never
heard? And how are they to hear without someone to proclaim
him? And how are they to proclaim him unless they are sent?

To ponder

I am here to tell you, people are hungry. And you have a feast
entrusted to you, and they are ready for it. —Nadia Bolz-Weber,
at 2012 ELCA Youth Gathering

Still hungry

Many studies and surveys tell us that people don't care much about religion anymore. Everyone is getting on just fine without God, thank you very much. But I don't believe it. I look around and I see people are not getting along fine at all. The god many people think they can do without is not the God I know. People who preach an angry and judging god are not afraid to share their faith. *That* is the religion people reject. But people are not doing fine.

There is a hunger for unconditional love and a yearning for freedom from the superficiality and self-absorption of this age. How can people know about this love if we do not share it? What would happen if we let our love shine brighter than the hate and condemnation so many associate with "religion"? I think we would be amazed.

Prayer

Dear God, show me today just one person who is yearning to know your love, and let my words and actions show them who you really are. Amen.

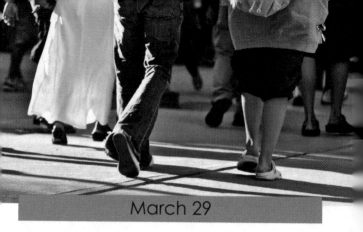

March 29

Romans 10:15b-17

As it is written, "How beautiful are the feet of those who bring good news!" But not all have obeyed the good news; for Isaiah says, "Lord, who has believed our message?" So faith comes from what is heard, and what is heard comes through the word of Christ.

To ponder

I believe that by my own understanding or strength I cannot believe in Jesus Christ my Lord or come to him, but instead the Holy Spirit has called me through the gospel, enlightened me with his gifts, made me holy and kept me in the true faith.
—Martin Luther, Small Catechism

Getting the word out

We are in a kind of partnership with God when it comes to faith. Make no mistake, faith is not something we can muster up on our own, it is a gift that comes only from the Holy Spirit. But the Holy Spirit doesn't just go around plopping faith into people. Faith comes from what is heard.

It may not be the most efficient delivery system, but the Holy Spirit uses us to bring others to faith. Being reluctant to talk about our faith is as old as the women at the empty tomb in Mark's gospel who "said nothing to anyone" after the angels instructed them to share the good news of Christ's resurrection (Mark 16:8). And yet the word got out, didn't it?

God is going to get the good news out, whether we go along with it or not. But wouldn't you rather be part of it?

Prayer

Dear God, who will hear the good news of your love from me today? Who will receive faith because your Holy Spirit showed your love through me? Give me trust to keep sharing your love, even when the answers to these and other questions remain a mystery. Amen.

March 30 / Lent 4

Romans 12:1-2

I appeal to you therefore, brothers and sisters, by the mercies of God, to present your bodies as a living sacrifice, holy and acceptable to God, which is your spiritual worship. Do not be conformed to this world, but be transformed by the renewing of your minds, so that you may discern what is the will of God— what is good and acceptable and perfect.

To ponder

We are each made for goodness, love and compassion. Our lives are transformed as much as the world is when we live with these truths. —Desmond Tutu, in *Huffington Post*

Living is loving

We are made for goodness, love, and compassion. So much angst is created trying to discern "God's will for me," but really this is God's will for us—goodness and compassion. How and where we live that out is really up to us. This is what it means to present our bodies as living sacrifices before God. There's no secret map God has laid out that we have to decipher. God has made us for goodness, love, and compassion.

God has given us a whole world to explore and different gifts to use in the service of love and compassion. The paths we choose to show that love and goodness are the living sacrifices we present before God. As we live out that goodness, love, and compassion God has created us for, not only do we become more loving and compassionate, but so does the world around us. This is how God makes us good and acceptable and perfect.

Prayer

Dear God, show me how to be good and loving and compassionate today, so that I may be transformed and also transform the world around me. Amen.

March 31

Romans 12:3-5

For by the grace given to me I say to everyone among you not to think of yourself more highly than you ought to think, but to think with sober judgment, each according to the measure of faith that God has assigned. For as in one body we have many members, and not all the members have the same function, so we, who are many, are one body in Christ, and individually we are members one of another.

To ponder

We've been deceived by the thought that we would be more pleasing to God in our own way than in the way God has given us. —Catherine of Siena, *Letters*

All gifted

There is a kind of fake humility that passes itself off as piety but is really arrogance. It is the fake humility that says "I have nothing to offer."

Everyone has something to offer. Scripture says that over and over. To deny that this applies to me is to think more highly of myself than I ought to. Really? God gave *everyone* gifts but me? I may think that when I say I have nothing to offer I am being humble, but in truth I am being arrogant, lazy, and selfish. This thinking says "I know better than God what is needed." This thinking keeps me from doing the work God has called me to and keeps to myself the gifts God has given me for the sake of others.

Do I trust God or not? Didn't God know what God was doing—giving me the particular gifts I have? Putting me where these gifts are needed? Who am I going to trust, God or my own fears?

Prayer

Dear God, give me courage to say Yes! today to using the gifts you have given me for the sake of others. Amen.

April 1

Romans 12:6-8

We have gifts that differ according to the grace given to us: prophecy, in proportion to faith; ministry, in ministering; the teacher, in teaching; the exhorter, in exhortation; the giver, in generosity; the leader, in diligence; the compassionate, in cheerfulness.

To ponder

A compassionate community of Christ will not be worrying about being an eye or an ear or a little toe. The community will not be judging or envious, but will earnestly seek to discover the gifts of each member. This is one of the ways we love one another. —Mary R. Schramm, *Gifts of Grace*

Equal isn't equal

Equality before God doesn't mean we are all the same or have the same gifts. It's a fact some people are more gifted than others. However, the person with more gifts or one superior gift is not better or more loved than anyone else. We should be grateful for those gifts, not envious or resentful. And if we happen to be exceptionally gifted in one or more areas, we should be grateful, not embarrassed, for what we have.

Grace is what frees us from keeping score and making comparisons. It's not about us. It's about God and what God is doing among us so that more people experience grace.

Prayer

Dear God, thank you for all the ways my life is enhanced because of the gifts you have given others. Move me to better use the gifts you've given me so that others may experience your grace. Amen.

April 2

Romans 12:9-11

Let love be genuine; hate what is evil, hold fast to what is good;
love one another with mutual affection; outdo one another in
showing honor. Do not lag in zeal, be ardent in spirit, serve the
Lord.

To ponder

I choose love. . . . No occasion justifies hatred; no injustice war-
rants bitterness. I choose love. Today I will love God and what
God loves. —Max Lucado, *Let the Journey Begin*

Choose love

The love that scripture speaks of is not an emotion. It is a choice. We don't create love, it comes from God, but we can choose love over hate. Paul tells us to hate evil, but what is evil other than hate? So hate hate if you must hate, but hold fast to what is good. And there is plenty of good in the world. Where there is God, there is love, and where there is love there is good. The more we turn toward love, the more we love and the more goodness we see around us.

If you want to compete, try being the one who loves the most, who lifts up your neighbor the most. Be the one who sees the most good. Be the first to see what is good and hopeful in difficult situations. Be the first to point to the light in the darkness. Choose love today.

Prayer

Dear God, today let me be the one who loves the most, who gives in first, who says thanks first, who sees the good in someone that others have missed. Let me choose love today. Amen.

April 3

Romans 12:12-13

Rejoice in hope, be patient in suffering, persevere in prayer.
Contribute to the needs of the saints; extend hospitality to
strangers.

To ponder

"I mean . . . the point of church isn't to get people to come to
church." "No?" said Steve, cocking an eyebrow. "What is it?" It
seemed obvious to me. "To feed them, so they can go out and,
you know, be Jesus." —Sara Miles, *Take This Bread*

Be Jesus

"Be patient in suffering, persevere in prayer." Boy, that is something I don't want to hear. I pray all right, but it is not a patient prayer. "God, take care of this *now*" is my go-to prayer in difficulty.

How can we be patient in suffering? Paul tells us how. "Contribute to the needs of the saints." Take care of others. Think about someone other than yourself. I'm not the only one in the world with troubles, and certainly my troubles aren't worse than anyone else's.

I remember a homebound elderly saint I used to visit. She was nearly immobilized with arthritic pain, and yet when I visited all she wanted to talk about was who was suffering in the congregation and needed her prayers. This made her a kind and cheerful person who was always rejoicing in hope, despite her suffering. How can we rejoice in hope and be patient in suffering? By going out and being Jesus. By feeding others so they can go out and be Jesus.

Prayer

Dear God, you know all my troubles; I've certainly complained to you about them enough. Today let me put my own troubles aside so that I can feed another person, so that she or he can then go out and be Jesus. Amen.

Romans 12:14-16

Bless those who persecute you; bless and do not curse them. Rejoice with those who rejoice, weep with those who weep. Live in harmony with one another; do not be haughty, but associate with the lowly; do not claim to be wiser than you are.

To ponder

Too few rejoice at a friend's good fortune. —Aeschylus, *Agamemnon*

Sharing joy

I wonder if of all Paul's exhortations, this one is not often the most difficult: rejoice with those who rejoice. "Misery loves company," says the old adage. Usually it is not difficult to commiserate with someone who is suffering. Sometimes I can even muster up some sympathy for the suffering of someone I don't like. Being genuinely happy for someone whose life is going way better than mine, though, is another story. Envy and jealousy rear their ugly heads when my friends achieve success; worse is the bitterness that engulfs me when someone I don't like is happy.

But living in harmony is not just sharing sorrows. It's sharing joy as well. If I can remember what little I have done to deserve the good things that have come my way, I will stop worrying about whether or not my neighbors deserve their good fortune. When I am down and burdened with the cares of the world, rejoicing with others reminds me of the good things God has done and assures me that I too will one day invite others to rejoice with me.

Prayer

Dear God, help me step out of my preoccupation with my own life to genuinely rejoice and give thanks for the joys of my neighbors. Amen.

Romans 12:17-18

Do not repay anyone evil for evil, but take thought for what is noble in the sight of all. If it is possible, so far as it depends on you, live peaceably with all.

To ponder

Man must evolve for all human conflict a method which rejects revenge, aggression, and retaliation. The foundation of such a method is love. —Martin Luther King Jr., accepting 1964 Nobel Peace Prize

Windows to peace

"Two wrongs don't make a right." It was one of my dad's favorite phrases when we kids tried to defend ourselves against blame. Someone else had started it, we would say. Kay popped my balloon, so I drew a big crayon X on her picture. Retribution was justice! That was not the way Dad saw it. Two wrongs don't make a right.

Paul says, "Do not repay anyone evil for evil." When we are wronged it is easy to want to lash out. Payback seems natural and justified. Christians are called to something better. We ask ourselves, "What would the high road look like in this situation?"

In the face of hurtful action, what might we do that is good? We do not excuse the actions of those who have done harm, but neither do we descend to their level of human interaction. Instead, we follow Christ, who lived peaceably and who offered healing and forgiveness to others, even in the midst of the plot to bring about his death.

Prayer

Jesus, thank you for giving us an example of love in the midst of hate. Give us grace to follow you in all circumstances and to share your goodness and peace with everyone. Amen.

April 6 / Lent 5

Romans 13:8-10

Owe no one anything, except to love one another; for the one who loves another has fulfilled the law. The commandments, "You shall not commit adultery; You shall not murder; You shall not steal; You shall not covet"; and any other commandment, are summed up in this word, "Love your neighbor as yourself." Love does no wrong to a neighbor; therefore, love is the fulfilling of the law.

To ponder

"Being neighbor" to someone suggests a personal response drawn from my own resources. It involves practical expressions of love, justice, and hospitality. My responsibility to others is not limited by my immediate proximity to them. Grave need cries

out for response when help is within my power. . . . Neighborly hearts see with eyes of love and find ways to respond to the person next door, on the street downtown, and half a world away.
—Christine D. Pohl, *Living Pulpit*

Protective love

When you are a teenager and your parents impose rules, it is easy to believe they are against you. They have power over you, so they make curfews. They insist that you help around the house. They intervene in arguments you have with your siblings. Why do your parents do these things? When you are fifteen you might answer, "Just because they can."

When God commands things, is it just because God can? Is it that God likes to order people around, or that God is always looking for ways to spoil a party? No. Paul says, "Love does no wrong to a neighbor; therefore, love is the fulfilling of the law." Many of us have heard the news that God loves us, and we are grateful for that love. What we may not have heard as much is that God loves our neighbor too, just as much as God loves us.

Just as parents' rules are often intended to protect their children, God's law is intended to protect us and our neighbor. When we keep the commandments, we are acting out God's love for others. When we act in love toward others, we fulfill the law.

Prayer

Gracious God, help us to feel your love for us and share your love with our neighbors. Amen.

Romans 13:11-12

Besides this, you know what time it is, how it is now the moment for you to wake from sleep. For salvation is nearer to us now than when we became believers; the night is far gone, the day is near. Let us then lay aside the works of darkness and put on the armor of light.

To ponder

This is what God wakes us up to do. God calls on us to work together in small ways to let God's light shine brightly in a great way. This is what it means to face the world. We look at our little corner of the world and we see how we can make a difference where we are, in our own ways. In order to get to this point we first have to wake up, and then we have to get up. —N. Graham Standish, *Paradoxes for Living*

Eager waiting

Think of something you have eagerly waited for. Maybe it was your birthday, or permission to drive the family car. Maybe you have been eager to dive into a new job, or impatient for a dear friend's visit. As you wait, your excitement bubbles over into action. You help plan a party. You "practice" driving a parked car. You buy a new lunch bag, even though the job is still two weeks away. You ready the house for company.

Waiting for the return of Christ is something like these experiences. Even before Christ's return, our expectation of that event changes the way we live. For Christians, waiting looks like honorable living. To "put on the armor of light" is to live in the new day before it has dawned, just as when the birthday girl tries on her party dress days before she actually needs to wear it, or when someone expecting a houseguest prepares the guest's favorite foods before anyone has arrived. By works of love for God and neighbor, we get ready to receive our Lord Jesus Christ with joy.

Prayer

Lord Jesus, grant that our waiting for you might overflow in service to others. Amen.

April 8

Romans 14:5-6

Some judge one day to be better than another, while others judge all days to be alike. Let all be fully convinced in their own minds. Those who observe the day, observe it in honor of the Lord. Also those who eat, eat in honor of the Lord, since they give thanks to God; while those who abstain, abstain in honor of the Lord and give thanks to God.

To ponder

God will find a way to let us know he is with us *in this place*, wherever we are. . . . And maybe that's one reason we worship—to respond to grace. We praise God not to celebrate our own faith but to give thanks for the faith God has in us. To let ourselves look at God, and let God look back at us. And to laugh, and sing, and be delighted because God has called us his own. —Kathleen Norris, *Amazing Grace*

Open practice

Is it better to open presents on Christmas Eve or Christmas Day? You probably have an opinion about that question, perhaps a strong opinion. Often we do not recognize our own traditions until someone new joins the family. Your college roommate comes home for a holiday and shares some of her family's traditions with you. Or a new in-law brings guacamole to Thanksgiving dinner, and after the initial confusion (What is it? How are we supposed to eat it?), everyone discovers it goes surprisingly well with turkey.

Likewise, in our Christian practice, we probably do things that are meaningful to us, but not necessary for every other Christian to do. We have particular ways of celebrating festivals, or perhaps we practice fasting as a means of prayer. While these things help some of us to live our faith in daily life, they are not necessary for all Christians. About such things, Paul says, basically, Whatever. The only thing necessary is to do what we do for the Lord. So we ask ourselves, Will this practice honor the Lord? If so, it need not be a matter of conflict among us.

Prayer

Lord Jesus, by becoming human and living among us, you honored all humanity. Help us to give you thanks and honor you in everything we do. Amen.

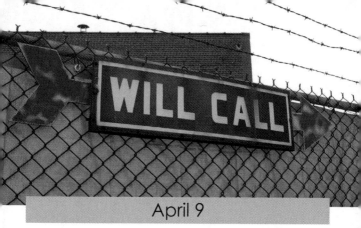

April 9

Romans 14:10-12

Why do you pass judgment on your brother or sister? Or you, why do you despise your brother or sister? For we will all stand before the judgment seat of God. For it is written,

"As I live, says the Lord, every knee shall bow to me,
and every tongue shall give praise to God."

So then, each of us will be accountable to God.

To ponder

Any parent, watching a child grow up, can see some weeds in the wheat. And while we try to teach a child right from wrong, when it comes to spotting those weeds and uprooting them, we can't be perfect ourselves and can't expect others to be. As the parable says, in pulling up the weeds, we risk pulling up good

74

wheat along with them. I began to find the parable absurdly freeing not from responsibility but from the disease of perfectionism. —Kathleen Norris, *Amazing Grace*

No judging

Most of us do not think of ourselves as judgmental, but the impulse may be nearer to us than we imagine. Perhaps we are sure of our political opinions and sure that the "other side" is destroying the things we love most. Maybe we are impatient with the way decisions are being made, and we are tempted to think that if only *that* person (the pastor? the congregation's president? the musician?) were not in the picture, everything would run smoothly. Or we are on the receiving end of judgment and resent the one who decided that we are the problem.

Paul reminds us that judgment is God's work, not ours. When Paul says God is judge, he does not mean that God will eventually turn out to be on our side and destroy our enemies. God's dream is not destruction but acknowledgment. "Every tongue shall give praise," says the prophet Isaiah. Even the people we are most tempted to condemn or dismiss will someday understand God's majesty and loving kindness and respond on bended knee. Can you imagine praising God alongside your enemy?

Prayer

Dear God, we praise you for the love you have shown us in Christ Jesus. Form that same love in us, that we may not judge or despise our brothers and sisters. Amen.

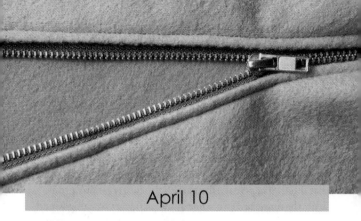

April 10

Romans 15:1-2

We who are strong ought to put up with the failings of the weak, and not to please ourselves. Each of us must please our neighbor for the good purpose of building up the neighbor.

To ponder

Love here is not a sentimental reaction, to be provoked simply by seeing a look of hurt or disappointment on someone else's face; it is rooted in the conviction that the Messiah died for the other person, too, and that, being oneself a beneficiary of his self-giving love, one cannot deliberately put a stumbling block in the way of another beneficiary. —N. T. Wright, in *New Interpreter's Bible*

Strength building

When you think of strength, what comes to mind? Body builders? Olympic athletes? The strong-willed toddler who has just learned the word *no*?

Years ago, I was part of a running club. When one particular runner was leading our group run, he would set the pace and stay with the front-runners. Then, at the end of the course, he would lead the early finishers back along the course to meet up with the rest of us. From there, the whole group would finish the run together at the slower runners' pace. The fast runners ran their best race and recorded their finish times on their watches, then they turned around, found the rest of us, and we all jogged across the finish line together. It didn't cost the fast runners anything, and it made us all feel like winners.

Strength, in the Christian life, is not demonstrated by the capacity to exercise power over others or by the practice of ignoring others while we stride far ahead of them. Christians show strength by building up the neighbor.

Prayer

Gracious God, your Son Jesus showed your power by becoming human, by living among us, and by following the way of the cross. Grant that we may feel his strength when we are weak, and use his strength to build up others. Amen.

April 11

Romans 15:4

For whatever was written in former days was written for our instruction, so that by steadfastness and by the encouragement of the scriptures we might have hope.

To ponder

These things were written that we might not fall away, for we have many battles to fight, both inward and outward. But being comforted by the Scriptures we can exhibit patience, so that by living in patience we might dwell in hope. For these things produce one another—hope brings forth patience and patience, hope. —John Chrysostom, *Homilies on Romans 27*

Old/new word

A woman who had lost two of her adult children to death once said to me, "Sometimes the only prayer you have is, 'My God, my God, why have you forsaken me?'" Her prayer, from Psalm 22, was once also the prayer of Jesus.

Just before today's verse from Romans, Paul has quoted a verse from the Psalms and used it to describe Jesus Christ's way in the world: "The insults of those who insult you have fallen on me" (Rom. 15:3; Ps. 69:9). The psalms are prayers for many different times and places. Both Psalm 22 and Psalm 69 tell the story of a faithful person enduring the unjust judgment of enemies and asking God for deliverance. After Paul's experience of the risen Christ, Paul saw in these old words a description of what Jesus endured in his suffering and death.

The scriptures give us words to address to God, characters to identify with, and stories to make sense of our lives. Old words speak to new times, and as they do, God's Spirit guides and encourages us. The words offer hope in the midst of the challenges in our life together.

Prayer

We thank you, O God, that you continue to speak to us through the holy scriptures. Grant that we may hear your word and trust in your promises. Amen.

April 12

Romans 15:5-6

May the God of steadfastness and encouragement grant you to live in harmony with one another, in accordance with Christ Jesus, so that together you may with one voice glorify the God and Father of our Lord Jesus Christ.

To ponder

In the end we shall have had enough of cynicism and skepticism and humbug, and we shall want to live—more musically.
—Vincent van Gogh, letter to brother Theo

A chord

If you sing or play an instrument, or even just like listening to music, you can probably guess what Paul means when he prays that the Romans might "live in harmony" with one another. Harmony is something different from just keeping a lid on conflict. To have harmony, you must have multiple notes in the air at the same time. Harmony is richer than one single melody line. Space opens up for major and minor chords, for dissonance, and for the resolution of dissonance.

How might our congregational life be different if we imagined our shared work to be creating a harmony that glorified God? Might we puzzle over things more creatively, realizing we did not have to rush to the resolution of chords into a single note? Together we could create chord structures none of us had imagined alone, but which are nonetheless beautiful. Dissonance could be part of the music. Notes different from our own would be vital to the whole, rather than disruptive and out of place.

Paul asks that God might fashion his readers into a people who praise God with complex and beautiful harmony.

Prayer

Dear God, by your Holy Spirit shape our congregations into places of harmony and praise for your glorious work to create, redeem, and sustain us and all that exists. Amen.

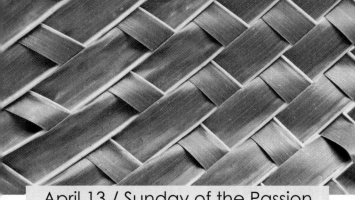

April 13 / Sunday of the Passion

Romans 14:7-9

We do not live to ourselves, and we do not die to ourselves. If we live, we live to the Lord, and if we die, we die to the Lord; so then, whether we live or whether we die, we are the Lord's. For to this end Christ died and lived again, so that he might be Lord of both the dead and the living.

To ponder

We are not our own, either as individuals or as a human race. This recognition humbles us; but it also give us hope that in our failures as well as in our successes, we belong to God. With the assurance that not even death will separate us from God's love, we can dare to nurture the Christian practices that will help each of us to embody God's mercy to one another while we live and then, when it is time, to die well. —Amy Plantinga Pauw, in *Practicing Our Faith*

Held for life

My first year of college was spent examining everything about my faith, my politics, my values, and my dreams for the future. Every day brought new information and experiences that I had to try to incorporate into what I thought I knew about the world. It was exhilarating, but also frightening. Sometimes I could make things fit together and sometimes I couldn't.

In the midst of all this upheaval, I was introduced to Paul's words in today's scripture reading. A congregation that I sometimes attended near my college would print Romans 14:8 in the bulletin every time a funeral was announced. We belong to God even in death.

The other part of the verse is just as important. The text's message to a young college student was something like this: "Your life, right now, is an arena in which God is active. Here and now, God is loving, restoring, and calling you to dive into love for God and neighbor with as much abandon as God did in Christ Jesus." To rest, work, and play in that embrace of God is to "live to the Lord."

Prayer

Christ Jesus, we commend ourselves to your care this day. Inspire in us the trust that nothing in life or death can separate us from you. Amen.

Romans 5:1-2

Therefore, since we are justified by faith, we have peace with God through our Lord Jesus Christ, through whom we have obtained access to this grace in which we stand; and we boast in our hope of sharing the glory of God.

To ponder

Lord, make us instruments of your peace. Where there is hatred, let us sow love; where there is injury, pardon; where there is discord, union; where there is doubt, faith; where there is despair, hope; where there is darkness, light; where there is sadness, joy. Grant that we may not so much seek to be consoled as to console; to be understood as to understand; to be loved as to love. For it is in giving that we receive; it is in pardoning that we are pardoned; and it is in dying that we are born to eternal life. Amen. —Prayer attributed to Francis of Assisi

Access point

Sometimes "peace" in a strained or broken relationship is not much more than an agreement to stay out of each other's way. Kids on a road trip draw an imaginary line down the center of the backseat. "You leave me alone and I'll leave you alone." Roommates wear themselves out arguing, and take refuge in opposite sides of the apartment. People at work just try to avoid a combative colleague. Isolation equals peace. Other times, peace means walking on pins and needles around someone. We do not isolate ourselves from them, but we are very careful lest we say something that will be interpreted as an insult.

Peace with God is different. It is neither disengagement from God nor carefulness born of fear. In fact, it is the opposite of these things. When Paul describes the peace that Christ brings us, he uses the words *access* and *sharing*. We are connected to God and to the favor God shows us in Christ. Peace with God is the joy of being in God's presence, without the fear of not measuring up.

Prayer

O God, conflict and fear continue to threaten justice, mercy, and peace in our lives and world. Draw all your children into community with you and into peace with one another. Make us instruments of your peace. Amen.

April 15

Romans 5:3-5

We also boast in our sufferings, knowing that suffering produces endurance, and endurance produces character, and character produces hope, and hope does not disappoint us, because God's love has been poured into our hearts through the Holy Spirit that has been given to us.

To ponder

Maybe the answer is to step off, to fling ourselves into the waiting arms of God, to be embraced by the Jesus who says, "I am all the endurance and character and hope you will ever need." When we insist that suffering have some meaning, that it produce something or mean something, we no longer need God. We've got the answers. And when we travel round and round that circle, we bog ourselves down with all the baggage that gets in the way of God doing God's work! —MaryAnn McKibben Dana, in *Journal for Preachers*

Not disappointed

In many ways this passage feels dismissive of suffering, as if Paul were counseling us, no matter what, to look on the bright side. It helps to remember that Paul himself knew suffering. He was rejected by many of his own people, beaten, imprisoned multiple times, and finally martyred. Paul is not theologizing on the abstract concept of suffering. He is trying to make sense of the twists and turns his own life has taken, and of the suffering that has been such a steady companion to him in his walk with Christ.

In the context of his own life, then, he says, "Hope does not disappoint us." His words are the testimony of one man who is able to endure suffering because he knows that Christ, the Crucified One, will embody God's love to him in the midst of it, and will see him through it.

Prayer

Lord Jesus, thank you for loving with a love that bears all things, believes all things, hopes all things, and endures all things. Form such love in us, that we may share it with others. Amen.

April 16

Romans 5:6-8

For while we were still weak, at the right time Christ died for the ungodly. Indeed, rarely will anyone die for a righteous person—though perhaps for a good person someone might actually dare to die. But God proves his love for us in that while we still were sinners Christ died for us.

To ponder

For the task and mission of evangelism, an often-neglected dynamic is telling people that there is a God who has been looking out for the interests of all of humankind and the world in which they live, even before they knew it. Evangelism is not just the beginning of a relationship with God. It is also the acknowledgement of God's prior relationship with humanity. . . . We were

sinners. We were not yet aware of our salvation. But salvation had already been accomplished, and completed, in Jesus Christ.
—James L. Jarrard, in *Review & Expositor*

Even you

A friend of mine tells the story of preaching a sermon about God's love being something real and particular, not an abstraction. The sermon related how God rejoiced in the whole creation and longed to know and be known by each of us. "God loves you," the pastor said, addressing the individuals in the congregation. After the sermon, someone said at the door, "Pastor, if you really knew me, you wouldn't say that about me."

God really knows us and still loves us. God knows what is lovely about us and what is decidedly unlovely. God did not and does not arrive at a decision to love us based on a catalog of our virtues and vices. Jesus reached out to people who were sick, to notorious sinners, to disciples who were slow to understand him and quick to desert him at the end. He laid down his life for friends and enemies alike. Jesus is our best visual aid for how God loves: across differences; in spite of weakness, disease, and sin; one person at a time; and faithfully, even at great cost. Thanks be to God!

Prayer

Gracious God, thank you for loving us before we knew it. Create in us new and generous hearts, so that we may love everyone whom you love. Amen.

April 17 / Maundy Thursday

Romans 5:10-11

For if while we were enemies, we were reconciled to God through the death of his Son, much more surely, having been reconciled, will we be saved by his life. But more than that, we even boast in God through our Lord Jesus Christ, through whom we have now received reconciliation.

To ponder

We were made not primarily that we may love God (though we were made for that too) but that God may love us, that we may become objects in which the Divine love may rest "well pleased." —C. S. Lewis, in *The Complete C. S. Lewis*

Forward

Christian theologians have lots of theories about how the death of Jesus is a saving, reconciling work of Christ on our behalf. Jesus refuses to flee danger or take up arms against it, and so finally the powers of sin and death fling everything they have at him. He absorbs all that hostility and, though it costs him his life, he leaves healing and reconciliation in place of destruction.

Paul would likely agree with all of that. "We were reconciled to God through the death of his Son."

Paul says more. "We will be saved by his life." The risen life of Christ is as important to Paul as the death of Christ. It would be difficult to imagine one without the other. The risen Jesus goes forward with us. Our future is secure in Christ. Centuries before Jesus' birth, God had said to his people, "For surely I know the plans I have for you, . . . to give you a future with hope" (Jer. 29:11). Christ's risen life is the first fruits of the future and hope that God has planned for us and all creation.

Prayer

Give us faith, O God, that we may live the life that your Son has opened up for us. Amen.

April 18 / Good Friday

Romans 5:18-19

Therefore just as one man's trespass led to condemnation for all, so one man's act of righteousness leads to justification and life for all. For just as by the one man's disobedience the many were made sinners, so by the one man's obedience the many will be made righteous.

To ponder

The design of Christ's new creation is far too grand, too inclusive to be restricted to what happens inside my soul. No nook or cranny of history is too small for its purpose, no cultural potential too large for its embrace. Being in Christ, we are part of a new movement by His grace, a movement rolling on toward the new heaven and new earth where all things are made right and where He is all in all. —Lewis B. Smedes, *Union with Christ*

World-altering

In the Greek story of Pandora's box, all the evils of the world are let loose with a single act by Pandora: she opens the lid of a box she has been told never to look into. She rushes to close the lid, but it's too late. One action has led to a whole different world.

Paul uses the same idea and applies it to Adam and to Christ. As a result of Adam's disobedience, told in Genesis 2, the trajectory of human history is forever changed. The world, now, is characterized by brokenness. We contribute to it, to be sure, but sin defined this realm before we came on the scene. It is just the way things are.

Jesus Christ's life and death also has the world-transforming quality of Pandora's box or Adam's act of disobedience, but unlike those two, what Jesus does transforms the whole creation toward good. The whole system has changed again. The work of Christ and his gifts are for everyone of every time and place. Jesus transforms creation so that our realm may be defined by righteousness, healing, and reconciliation with the one who created it.

Prayer

O God, heal our world, that all people may live in the love of your Son and that all creation may sing your praise. Amen.

April 19 / Resurrection of Our Lord

Romans 6:3-5

Do you not know that all of us who have been baptized into Christ Jesus were baptized into his death? Therefore we have been buried with him by baptism into death, so that, just as Christ was raised from the dead by the glory of the Father, so we too might walk in newness of life. For if we have been united with him in a death like his, we will certainly be united with him in a resurrection like his.

To ponder

We gather at the four rivers of paradise, on the waters of the flood, at the edge of the Red Sea, on the banks of the Jordan, and at this font in order to be immersed in the river, the flood, the sea of God's infinite life. —Samuel Torvend, in *Homilies for the Christian People*

Easter flood

This is the night, and we are there, when the sea is parted even as the hosts of Pharaoh try to hold back the revolution God has begun. But a highway to freedom runs through the heart of the sea, and who can turn back now?

This is the night! Some will be buried with Christ this night to rise with him toward the Father's glory. All of us who have passed through the baptismal flood know that we have been united together in Christ's life. And so we gather again, around the flame and font, to hear the old, old story that is both our beginning and our ending, our origin and our goal.

Yes, the earth is quaking and the stone is moving and the foundations of the earth are realigning. But do not be afraid. You will see the Risen One. He comes to greet you, to bring you to himself, to go before you. Out of the dark the first light of dawn brings new vision for all God's people. This is the night—the beginning of the day—and it is time to go with Christ, who leads the way.

Prayer

Blessed are you, O God. You have raised us to new life in you. Return us over and over to those baptismal waters for forgiveness, refreshment, and renewal. Amen.

Notes

March 5: Augustine, *Confessions* (Oxford, 1992), 3. **March 6:** Mother Teresa, "Mother Teresa Reflects on Working toward Peace," written for Markkula Center for Applied Ethics, Santa Clara (Calif.) University (2008). **March 7:** Julian of Norwich, *Showings* (Paulist, 1978), 168. **March 8:** Marianne Williamson, *Everyday Grace* (Riverhead, 2002), 12-13. **March 9:** Julian of Norwich, *Showings* (Paulist, 1978), 130, 133. **March 10:** Grace Adolphsen Brame, *Faith, the Yes of the Heart* (Augsburg, 1999), 12. **March 11:** Thomas Merton, *Thoughts in Solitude* (Noonday / Farrar, Straus and Giroux, 1956, 1958), 83. **March 12:** Marilynne Robinson, *Gilead* (Farrar, Straus and Giroux, 2004), 129. **March 13:** George Bernanos, *The Diary of a Country Priest* (Image / Doubleday, 1954), 233. **March 14:** Michael Downey, *Altogether Gift: A Trinitarian Spirituality* (Orbis, 2000), 103-104. **March 15:** Jürgen Moltmann, *The Source of Life* (Fortress Press, 1997), 72. **March 16:** Richard Rohr, "Language of Those Who Know," in *Richard's Daily Meditations* (blog), April 11, 2013 (Albuquerque, NM: Center for Action and Contemplation). **March 17:** Anne Lamott, *Help, Thanks, Wow: The Three Essential Prayers* (Riverhead / Penguin, 2012), 6-7. **March 18:** Frederick Buechner, *The Longing for Home: Recollections and Reflections* (HarperCollins, 1996), 126-127. **March 19:** Gerard Manley Hopkins, "God's Grandeur," in *Hopkins: Poems and Prose* (Knopf, 1995), 14. **March 20:** Thelma Hall, *Too Deep for Words: Rediscovering Lectio Divina* (Paulist, 1988), 47, 51. **March 21:** Julian of Norwich, *Revelations of Divine Love*, ch. 32. **March 22:** Theodore G. Tappert, trans. and ed., *Luther: Letters of Spiritual Counsel* (Westminster, 1960; Vancouver, BC: Regent College Publishing, 2003). **March 23:** Bono, keynote address at fifty-fourth National Prayer Breakfast, Washington, DC, Feb. 2, 2006. **March 24:** J. R. R. Tolkien, *The Lord of the Rings: The Fellowship of the Ring*, Book I, *The Shadow of the Past*, 50th anniv. ed. (Mariner, 2012). **March 25:** Irenaeus of Lyons, *Irenæus Against Heresies*, Book IV, ch. 39, 2. **March 26:** Nelson Mandela, *Long Walk to Freedom* (Little Brown & Co., 1994). **March 27:** Maya Angelou, *Wouldn't Take Nothing for My Journey Now* (Bantam / Random House, 1994), 34. **March 28:** Nadia Bolz-Weber, speaking at 2012 ELCA Youth Gathering. **March 29:** Martin Luther, Small Catechism, explanation, Apostles' Creed, Third Article, in *Evangelical Lutheran Worship*, 1162. **March 30:** Desmond Tutu, in *Huffington Post*, Jan. 12, 2012. **March 31:** Suzanne Noffke, trans., *Letters of Catherine of Siena*, 2nd ed., 2 vols. (Tempe: Arizona Center for Medieval and Renaissance Studies, 2000), Letter T340. **April 1:** Mary R. Schramm, *Gifts of Grace: Discovering Your Unique Abilities* (Augsburg Fortress, 1982), 48. **April 2:** Max Lucado, *Let the Journey Begin: God's Roadmap for New Beginnings* (J. Countryman / Thomas Nelson, 1999). **April 3:** Sara Miles, *Take This Bread: A Radical Conversion* (Ballentine / Random House, 2007). **April 4:** Aeschylus, *Agamemnon*. **April 5:** Martin Luther King Jr., speech accepting the Nobel Peace Prize, Dec. 11, 1964. **April 6:** Christine D. Pohl, "Neighbors: Our Circle of Care," in *Living Pulpit*, vol. 11, no. 3 (2002), 21. **April 7:** N. Graham Standish, *Paradoxes for Living: Cultivating Faith in Confusing Times* (Westminster John Knox, 2001), 90. **April 8:** Kathleen Norris, *Amazing Grace: A Vocabulary of Faith* (Riverhead, 1998), 151. **April 9:** Kathleen Norris, *Amazing Grace: A Vocabulary of Faith* (Riverhead, 1998), 317. **April 10:** N. T. Wright, "Romans" in *New Interpreter's Bible*, vol. 10 (Abingdon, 2002), 750. **April 11:** John Chrysostom, "Homilies on Romans 27," in Gerald L. Bray, ed., *Romans*, vol. 6 in *Ancient Christian Commentary on Scripture: New Testament* (InterVarsity Press, 1998), 354-55. **April 12:** Vincent Van Gogh, quoted in Naomi Margolis Maurer, *The Pursuit of Spiritual Wisdom: The Thought and Art of Vincent Van Gogh and Paul Gauguin* (Farleigh Dickinson, 1998), 35. **April 13:** Amy Plantinga Pauw, "Dying Well," in Dorothy C. Bass, ed., *Practicing Our Faith* (Jossey-Bass, 1997), 177. **April 14:** Prayer attributed to Francis of Assisi, in *Evangelical Lutheran Worship* (Augsburg Fortress, 2006), 87.